United States Government Accountability Office

Report to Congressional Committees

I0410964

August 2014

TROUBLED ASSET RELIEF PROGRAM

Government's Exposure to Ally Financial Lessens as Treasury's Ownership Share Declines

GAO-14-698

TROUBLED ASSET RELIEF PROGRAM

Government's Exposure to Ally Financial Lessens as Treasury's Ownership Share Declines

GAO Highlights

Highlights of GAO-14-698, a report to congressional committees

Why GAO Did This Study

As part of its Automotive Industry Financing Program, funded through the Troubled Asset Relief Program (TARP), Treasury provided $17.2 billion of assistance to Ally Financial (formerly known as GMAC). Ally Financial is a large financial holding company, the primary business of which is auto financing.

TARP's authorizing legislation mandates that GAO report every 60 days on TARP activities. This report examines (1) the status of Treasury's investments in Ally Financial and its efforts to wind down those investments and (2) the financial condition of Ally Financial.

To address these issues, GAO reviewed and analyzed available industry, financial, and regulatory data from 2009 through June 2014. GAO also reviewed rating agency analyses, Treasury reports and documentation detailing Treasury's investments in Ally Financial and its divestments from the company, as well as Ally Financial's financial filings and reports. GAO also interviewed officials from the Federal Deposit Insurance Corporation (FDIC), Federal Reserve, and Treasury, and representatives from Ally Financial.

GAO provided a draft of this report to FDIC, the Federal Reserve, Treasury, and Ally Financial. Treasury generally concurred with GAO's findings. Ally Financial provided technical comments, which GAO has incorporated, as appropriate. FDIC and the Federal Reserve did not provide comments.

GAO makes no recommendations in this report.

View GAO-14-698. For more information, contact A. Nicole Clowers at (202) 512-8678 or clowersa@gao.gov.

What GAO Found

The Department of the Treasury (Treasury) reduced its ownership stake in Ally Financial Inc. (Ally Financial) from 74 percent in October 2013, to 16 percent as of June 30, 2014. As shown in the figure below, the pace of Treasury's reduction in its ownership share of Ally Financial accelerated in 2013 and corresponds with two key events. First, in November 2013, the Board of Governors of the Federal Reserve System (Federal Reserve) did not object to Ally Financial's resubmitted 2013 capital plan, which allowed Ally Financial to repurchase preferred shares from Treasury and complete a private placement of common shares. Second, in December 2013 the bankruptcy proceedings of Ally Financial's mortgage subsidiary, Residential Capital LLC (ResCap), were substantially resolved. The confirmed Chapter 11 plan broadly released Ally Financial from any and all legal claims by ResCap and, subject to certain exceptions, all other third parties, in exchange for $2.1 billion in cash from Ally Financial and its insurers. As of June 30, 2014, Treasury had received $17.8 billion in sales proceeds and interest and dividend payments on its total assistance to Ally Financial of $17.2 billion.

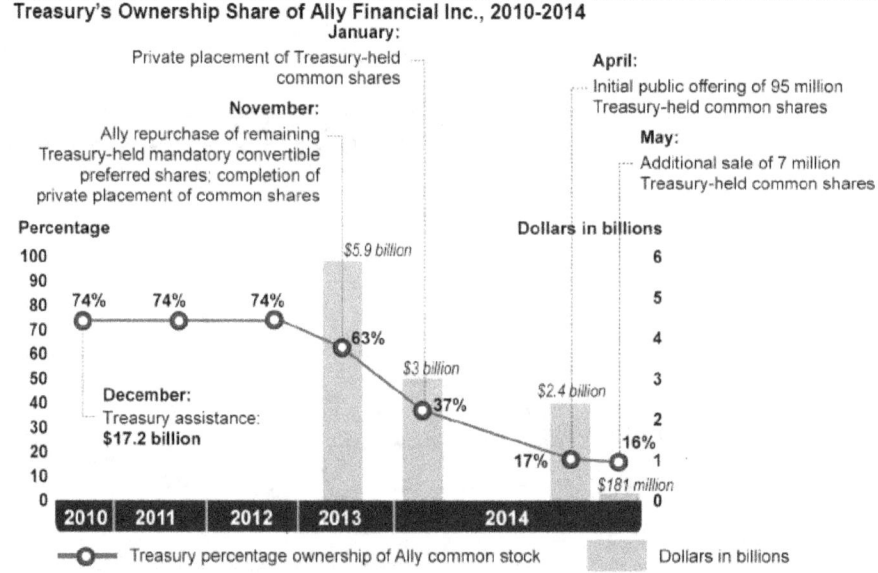

Treasury's Ownership Share of Ally Financial Inc., 2010-2014

Source: GAO summary of information from Treasury and Ally Financial Inc. | GAO-14-698

Ally Financial's financial condition has continued to stabilize in late 2013 and early 2014 as illustrated by multiple capital, profitability, and liquidity measures. For example, Ally Financial's capital ratios have remained above regulatory minimum levels since 2009, which indicates that it is in a better position to absorb financial losses. In addition, the company raised significant levels of common equity through private and public share offerings. According to recent credit rating agency analyses, Ally Financial is competitive in automotive financing, particularly in the floor-plan business segment, which focuses on dealer financing. However, analysts reported that the company faces potential competitive challenges, such as the loss of certain exclusive relationships with General Motors Company and Chrysler Group LLC.

_____ **United States Government Accountability Office**

Contents

Abbreviations

AIFP	Automotive Industry Financing Program
CCAR	Comprehensive Capital Analysis and Review
CPP	Capital Purchase Program
EESA	Emergency Economic Stabilization Act of 2008
FDIC	Federal Deposit Insurance Corporation
GM	General Motors Company
GMAC	General Motors Acceptance Corporation
IPO	initial public offering
ResCap	Residential Capital LLC
ROA	return on assets
SEC	Securities and Exchange Commission
TARP	Troubled Asset Relief Program

GAO U.S. GOVERNMENT ACCOUNTABILITY OFFICE

441 G St. N.W.
Washington, DC 20548

August 5, 2014

Congressional Committees

In 2008 and 2009, the Department of the Treasury (Treasury) provided significant support to the automotive industry—including automotive finance companies—after deteriorating economic conditions resulted in a dramatic decline in automobile sales and significant financial losses in the industry. Through the Automotive Industry Financing Program (AIFP) under the Troubled Asset Relief Program (TARP), Treasury provided $17.2 billion of assistance to GMAC LLC (General Motors Acceptance Corporation), a financial services company that provided consumer financing for vehicle purchases and dealer financing for inventory.[1] In 2010, GMAC became Ally Financial Inc. (Ally Financial).[2] As a result of its actions to provide assistance to the company, the federal government had an almost 74 percent interest in Ally Financial in 2010.

The Emergency Economic Stabilization Act of 2008 (EESA) provides GAO with broad oversight authorities for actions taken under TARP, including assistance under AIFP.[3] We have analyzed and monitored Treasury's activities in implementing TARP in a number of reports. More specifically, in our October 2013 report, we analyzed Treasury's assistance to Ally Financial and its efforts to wind down its investments.[4] This report examines (1) the status of Treasury's investments in Ally Financial as of June 30, 2014, and its efforts to wind down those

---

[1]Pub. L. No. 110-343, § 101, 122 Stat. 3765, 3767 (codified at 12 U.S.C. § 5211). The total amount disbursed includes $16.3 billion committed by Treasury directly to GMAC/Ally Financial as well as an $884 million Treasury loan to General Motors Corporation (GM) that Treasury exchanged for a 35.4 percent common ownership share in GMAC. This report focuses on Ally Financial and does not examine the assistance provided to other automobile manufacturers or auto financing companies through AIFP, including GM and Chrysler Group LLC.

[2]In 2009, GMAC expanded its depository banking operation under the name of Ally Bank. For activities and events that predate the name change, we refer to the company as GMAC.

[3]Pub. L. No. 110-343, § 116, 122 Stat. 3765, 3783 (codified at 12 U.S.C. § 5226).

[4]GAO, *Troubled Asset Relief Program: Status of Treasury's Investments in General Motors and Ally Financial*, GAO-14-6 (Washington, D.C.: Oct. 29, 2013).

investments and (2) the financial condition of Ally Financial through March 31, 2014.

To determine the status of Treasury's investments in Ally Financial, we reviewed Treasury's monthly reports to Congress detailing the levels of the investments made in the company, including the number of shares owned by Treasury, and Treasury's daily transactions reports.[5] To analyze Treasury's efforts to wind down those investments, we reviewed Treasury documentation relating to its exit from Ally Financial. We reviewed Ally Financial regulatory filings, including Securities and Exchange Commission (SEC) filings; and publicly available reports from the Board of Governors of the Federal Reserve System (Federal Reserve) on its 2014 stress tests of bank holding companies and 2014 Comprehensive Capital Analysis and Review (CCAR).[6] We also interviewed officials from Treasury, Federal Reserve, Federal Deposit Insurance Corporation (FDIC), and representatives from Ally Financial. To assess the financial condition of Ally Financial, we measured the institution's capital ratios, net income, net interest spread margin, return on assets, nonperforming asset ratio, liquidity ratio, bank deposits, and operating cash flow, generally from 2009 through the first quarter (March 31) of 2014. We obtained these data from SNL Financial, a provider of financial information. We also reviewed reports by several credit rating agencies on how they rate Ally Financial's financial strength. We assessed the completeness and accuracy of all data used in this report and determined they were sufficiently reliable for the purposes of this report. For a more detailed discussion of the scope and methodology, see appendix I.

---

[5]Under EESA, every 30 days, Treasury must submit to Congress reports on TARP-related actions taken and funds obligated and spent during the reporting period as well as detailed financial statements that include agreements made, assets purchased, and transactions realized, and the valuation or pricing method used for each transaction. § 105(a), 122 Stat. at 3771-72 (codified at 12 U.S.C. § 5215).

[6]Stress testing helps bank supervisors measure whether a bank holding company has enough capital to support its operations throughout periods of stress. The Dodd-Frank Wall Street Reform and Consumer Protection Act (Dodd-Frank Act) requires the Federal Reserve to perform an annual stress test of bank holding companies with $50 billion or more in total consolidated assets. Pub. L. No. 111-203, § 165(i)(1)(A), 124 Stat. 1376, 1430 (2010)(codified at 12 U.S.C. § 5365(i)(1)(A)). CCARs are the Federal Reserve's annual assessments of the internal capital planning process and capital adequacy of large, complex U.S. bank holding companies. 12 C.F.R. § 225.8.

GAO-14-698 Troubled Asset Relief Program

We conducted this performance audit from March 2014 to August 2014 in accordance with generally accepted government auditing standards. Those standards require that we plan and perform the audit to obtain sufficient, appropriate evidence to provide a reasonable basis for our findings and conclusions based on our audit objectives. We believe that the evidence obtained provides a reasonable basis for our findings based on our audit objectives.

Background

Ally Financial is one of the country's largest financial holding companies, with total assets of $148.5 billion as of March 31, 2014.[7] Its primary line of business is automotive financing—both consumer financing and leasing and dealer floor-plan financing.[8] Ally Financial (when it was known as GMAC) formerly served as General Motors Company's (GM) captive automotive finance company.[9] GMAC's subsidiaries offered financial services such as auto insurance and residential mortgages. In 2006, Cerberus Capital Management purchased 51 percent of the company (GM retained 49 percent). As the housing market declined in the late 2000s, the previously profitable GMAC mortgage business unit began producing significant losses. For example, the company's Residential Capital LLC (ResCap) subsidiary lost approximately $17 billion from 2007 through 2009. During the same period, U.S. automobile sales dropped from 16.4 million to 10.4 million cars and light trucks, negatively affecting the company's core automobile financing business. On May 14, 2012, ResCap and certain of its wholly owned direct and indirect subsidiaries

---

[7]Ally Financial is a bank holding company that elected to become a financial holding company in December 2013. A financial holding company is a bank holding company that is allowed to engage in a broad range of financial activities, including securities underwriting and dealing, insurance underwriting, and merchant banking activities. Ally Financial was the twentieth-largest bank holding company in the United States as of March 31, 2014.

[8]Floor-plan, or wholesale, financing is a form of retail goods inventory financing in which each loan advance is made against a specific piece of collateral. As each piece of collateral is sold by the dealer, the loan advance against that piece of collateral is repaid or other acceptable collateral is substituted. Items commonly subject to floor-plan debt include automobiles, large home appliances, furniture, television and stereo equipment, boats, and mobile homes.

[9]A captive automotive lender's primary business is to finance the purchase of a specific manufacturer's automobiles. Prior to bankruptcy reorganization, GM's legal name was General Motors Corporation. General Motors Company is a new legal entity created through the bankruptcy process to purchase the operating assets of the prereorganization company.

filed voluntary petitions for relief under Chapter 11 of the Bankruptcy Code in the U.S. Bankruptcy Court for the Southern District of New York (Bankruptcy Court). The bankruptcy created uncertainties about Ally Financial's financial obligations.

Regulation and Supervision of Ally Financial

As a financial holding company, Ally Financial is regulated and supervised by the Federal Reserve.[10] Under the Dodd-Frank Act and implementing regulations, the Federal Reserve conducts an annual supervisory stress test of bank holding companies with $50 billion or more in total consolidated assets to evaluate whether the companies have sufficient capital to absorb losses resulting from adverse economic conditions. For the stress tests, the Federal Reserve projects revenue, expenses, losses, and resulting post-test capital levels, and regulatory capital ratios, including the tier 1 capital ratio and the tier 1 common ratio, under three economic scenarios (baseline, adverse, and severely adverse).[11] In addition, the Federal Reserve requires the same bank holding companies to conduct an annual company-run stress test using the same macroeconomic scenarios that the Federal Reserve uses to conduct its supervisory stress test.

---

[10] 12 U.S.C. § 1844(b)-(c).

[11] Tier 1 capital is currently considered the most stable and readily available capital that a banking institution can have to support its operations by absorbing unexpected financial losses. It consists of core capital elements, such as common stockholders' equity and noncumulative perpetual preferred stock. As defined in the Federal Reserve's Risk-Based Capital Adequacy Guidelines, tier 1 capital is composed of common and non-common equity elements, some of which are subject to limits on their inclusion in tier 1 capital. See 12 CFR § 225, Appendix A, § II.A.1. These elements include common stockholders' equity, qualifying perpetual preferred stock, certain minority interests, and trust preferred securities. Certain intangible assets, including goodwill and deferred tax assets, are deducted from tier 1 capital or are included subject to limits. See 12 CFR § 225, Appendix A, § II.B. Tier 1 common capital is tier 1 capital less the non-common elements of tier 1 capital, including perpetual preferred stock and related surplus, minority interest in subsidiaries, trust preferred securities, and mandatory convertible preferred securities. 12 CFR § 225.8(c)(10). Common equity is considered the most loss-absorbing form of capital. In July 2013, the federal banking regulators issued revised requirements for minimum capital, regulatory capital, and additional capital "buffers" to enhance the resiliency of banking organizations during periods of financial stress. These new standards will be implemented over multiple years. Regulatory Capital Rules: Regulatory Capital, Implementation of Basel III, Capital Adequacy, Transition Provisions, Prompt Corrective Action, Standardized Approach for Risk-Weighted Assets, Market Discipline and Disclosure Requirements, Advanced Approaches Risk-Based Capital Rule, and Market Risk Capital Rule, 78 Fed. Reg. 62019 (Oct. 11, 2013) (Federal Reserve and Office of the Comptroller of the Currency); 78 Fed. Reg. 55340 (Sept. 10, 2013) (FDIC).

The Federal Reserve also conducts an annual exercise, CCAR, to help ensure that large bank holding companies have robust, forward-looking capital planning processes that take into account their unique risks and set aside sufficient capital to operate during periods of economic and financial stress.[12] The Federal Reserve evaluates capital adequacy; internal processes for assessing capital adequacy; plans for capital distributions, such as dividend payments or stock repurchases; and other actions that affect capital.[13]

The Federal Reserve may object to a capital plan because of significant deficiencies in the planning process or because one or more capital ratios would fall below required levels under the assumption of stress and planned distributions.[14] If the Federal Reserve objects to a proposed capital plan, the bank holding company is permitted to make capital distributions only if the Federal Reserve indicates in writing that it does not object.[15] The company also must resubmit the capital plan after remediating the deficiencies.[16]

In March 2013, the Federal Reserve reported the results of its 2013 supervisory stress test and of the CCAR exercise.[17] The Federal Reserve

---

[12]In November 2011, the Federal Reserve issued a regulation requiring large bank holding companies to submit an annual capital plan. Capital Plans, 76 Fed. Reg. 74631 (Dec. 1, 2011) (codified at 12 C.F.R. § 225.8).

[13]12 C.F.R. § 225.8(d).

[14]12 C.F.R. § 225.8(e)(2)(ii). A capital distribution is defined as a redemption or repurchase of any debt or equity capital instrument, a payment of common or preferred stock dividends, a payment that may be temporarily or permanently suspended by the issuer on any instrument that is eligible for inclusion in the numerator of any minimum regulatory capital ratio, and any similar transaction that the Federal Reserve determines to be in substance a distribution of capital. 12 C.F.R. § 225.8(c)(2) .

[15]12 C.F.R. § 225.8(e)(2)(iv)

[16]12 C.F.R. § 225.8(d)(4).

[17]In 2013, 18 bank holding companies were subject to stress tests and to CCAR. These were Ally Financial Inc., American Express Company, Bank of America Corporation, The Bank of New York Mellon Corporation, BB&T Corporation, Capital One Financial Corporation, Citigroup Inc., Fifth Third Bancorp, The Goldman Sachs Group, Inc., JPMorgan Chase & Co., KeyCorp, Morgan Stanley, The PNC Financial Services Group, Inc., Regions Financial Corporation, State Street Corporation, Sun Trust Banks, Inc., U.S. Bancorp, and Wells Fargo & Co. The same 18 bank holding companies subject to the stress tests were subject to CCAR. In 2013, the Federal Reserve expanded to 30 the number of bank holding companies subject to stress tests and CCAR.

found that Ally Financial's tier 1 common capital ratio fell below the required 5 percent under the severely adverse scenario. Ally Financial was the only one of the 18 bank holding companies tested that fell below this required level. The Federal Reserve objected to Ally Financial's capital plan during the 2013 CCAR.[18] According to the Federal Reserve, Ally Financial's capital ratios did not meet the required minimums under the proposed capital plan. Specifically, the Federal Reserve reported that under stress conditions, Ally Financial's plan resulted in a tier 1 common ratio of 1.52 percent, which is below the required level of 5 percent under the capital plan rule. According to the Federal Reserve CCAR results paper, these results assumed that Ally Financial remained subject to contingent liabilities associated with ResCap. The Federal Reserve required Ally Financial to resubmit its capital plan, which Ally Financial did in September 2013.

Ally Financial owns Ally Bank, an Internet- and telephone-based bank. Ally Bank is a state-chartered nonmember bank supervised by FDIC and the Utah Department of Financial Institutions. Ally Bank had more than $55.9 billion in total deposits as of March 31, 2014.

Treasury Assistance through TARP

To help stabilize the automotive industry and avoid further economic disruptions, Treasury disbursed $79.7 billion through AIFP from December 2008 through June 2009. The assistance was used to support two automakers, Chrysler and GM, and their automotive finance companies, Chrysler Financial and GMAC.[19] In July 2009, Treasury outlined guiding principles for the investments, including

- exiting its investments as soon as practicable in a timely and orderly manner that minimizes financial market and economic impact;

- protecting taxpayer investment and maximizing overall investment returns within competing constraints;

---

[18]Of the 18 bank holding companies reviewed in 2013, the Federal Reserve also objected to one other company's capital plans.

[19]Before the bankruptcy reorganization, Chrysler's legal name was Chrysler LLC. Chrysler Group LLC is a new legal entity created through the bankruptcy process to purchase the operating assets of the prereorganization company.

GAO-14-698 Troubled Asset Relief Program

- improving the strength and viability of GM and Chrysler so that they could contribute to economic growth and jobs without government involvement; and

- managing its ownership stake in a hands-off, commercial manner, including voting its shares only on core governance issues, such as the selection of a company's board of directors and major corporation events or transactions.[20]

In late December 2008, as a part of AIFP, Treasury agreed to purchase $5 billion in senior preferred equity from GMAC and received an additional $250 million in preferred shares through warrants that Treasury exercised immediately.[21]

Treasury subsequently provided GMAC with additional assistance through TARP.

- In May 2009, Treasury purchased $7.5 billion of mandatory convertible preferred shares from GMAC. Also, in May 2009, Treasury exercised its option to exchange an $884 million loan to GM for a 35.4 percent common ownership share in GMAC.[22]

- In December 2009, Treasury made additional investments in Ally Financial—$2.5 billion of trust preferred securities and approximately

---

[20]Treasury established two other programs under AIFP—the Auto Supplier Support Program and the Auto Warranty Commitment Program. The Auto Supplier Support Program was designed to ensure that automakers received the parts and components they needed to manufacture vehicles and that suppliers had access to liquidity on their receivables. Under this program, GM and Chrysler received loans, all of which have been repaid. The Auto Warranty Commitment Program was designed to mitigate consumer uncertainty about purchasing vehicles from the restructuring automakers by providing funding to guarantee the warranties on new vehicles from those automakers. Funds were provided to GM and Chrysler under this program, but both companies were able to continue to honor consumer warranties and the funds have been repaid in full.

[21]GMAC applied to participate in the TARP Capital Purchase Program (CPP), but, as a commercial company, was not initially eligible for assistance. To become eligible, GMAC sought to convert its charter from an industrial loan company to a commercial bank in 2008 and applied to the Federal Reserve for bank holding company status. GMAC also submitted an application to participate in CPP, conditional upon becoming a bank holding company. The Federal Reserve approved GMAC's bank holding company application in December 2008. However, GMAC did not participate in CPP.

[22]Mandatory convertible preferred stock is a type of preferred share that must be converted to common stock on or before a certain contractual date.

$1.3 billion of mandatory convertible preferred shares.[23] Also, in December 2009, Treasury converted $3 billion of existing mandatory convertible preferred shares into common stock, increasing its common equity ownership from 35 to 56.3 percent.

- In December 2010, Treasury converted $5.5 billion of existing mandatory convertible preferred shares into common stock, increasing its common equity ownership to approximately 74 percent of Ally Financial.[24]

Ally Financial announced a plan in 2012 to repurchase Treasury's mandatory convertible preferred shares, worth $5.9 billion, to reduce Treasury's investment in the company. However, this plan stalled after the Federal Reserve objected to Ally Financial's initial 2013 capital plan submission, partly because of uncertainty about the company's obligations associated with the ResCap bankruptcy.

Resolution of Major Regulatory and Legal Issues Was Key to Treasury Reducing Its Ownership Share in Ally Financial

Two key regulatory and legal developments allowed Ally Financial and Treasury to move ahead with plans to reduce Treasury's investments in the company in late 2013. First, in November 2013, the Federal Reserve did not object to Ally Financial's resubmitted capital plan. Second, in December 2013, the bankruptcy proceedings of Ally Financial's mortgage subsidiary, ResCap, were substantially resolved. Following the resolution of these issues, Treasury significantly reduced its ownership stake in Ally Financial—primarily through sales of common stock—from 74 to 16 percent as of June 30, 2014. Also as of June 30, 2014, Treasury had received $17.8 billion (including interest and dividends), which exceeds the total Treasury assistance to the company of $17.2 billion.[25]

---

[23]A trust preferred security is a security that has both equity and debt characteristics, and is created by establishing a trust and issuing debt to it. The Dodd-Frank Act restricted the use of such securities in meeting certain capital requirements. Pub. L. No. 111-203, § 171, 124 Stat. 1376, 1435 (2010).

[24]In March 2011, Treasury received approximately $2.7 billion in proceeds from the sale of Ally Financial trust preferred securities.

[25]Treasury assistance to Ally Financial of $17.2 billion included $16.3 billion committed directly to GMAC/Ally Financial as well as the $884 million GM loan to Ally Financial that Treasury funded. The $17.8 billion that Treasury received from Ally Financial represents gross proceeds before deduction of commissions for sale of Ally Financial stock.

Resolution of Regulatory and Legal Issues Removed Uncertainty about Ally Financial

Two key regulatory and legal developments in the second half of 2013 helped Treasury accelerate the wind-down of its investments in Ally Financial.

- **Federal Reserve did not object to Ally Financial's resubmitted capital plan:** In November 2013 Ally Financial received a "nonobjection" from the Federal Reserve to its resubmitted 2013 CCAR capital plan, which enabled Ally Financial to move forward on its repurchase of $5.9 billion of the remaining Treasury-owned mandatory convertible preferred shares. As we previously reported, Treasury and Ally Financial agreed in August 2013 that Ally would repurchase the mandatory convertible preferred shares, conditioned on receiving a nonobjection on the resubmitted capital plan and the closing of a private placement securities transaction.[26] Ally Financial resubmitted its plan in September 2013 and the Federal Reserve approved it on November 15, 2013. The Federal Reserve nonobjection enabled Ally Financial to complete the private placement of common shares valued at $1.3 billion announced in August 2013. The private placement, intended in part to help finance the repurchase of the $5.9 billion remaining Treasury-owned mandatory convertible preferred shares, was completed in November 2013, as was the repurchase of the Treasury shares. More recently, Ally Financial received a nonobjection from the Federal Reserve in March 2014 on its annual capital plan.[27]

---

[26]GAO-14-6. During 2013, Ally Financial completed the sale of its international automobile finance businesses, with the exception of its joint venture in China, which the company expects to complete in 2014 depending on the pace of government approvals in China.

[27]In 2014, the Federal Reserve conducted stress tests and reviewed capital plans under its CCAR for 30 bank holding companies. These companies were Ally Financial Inc.; American Express Company; Bank of America Corporation; The Bank of New York Mellon Corporation; BB&T Corporation; BBVA Compass Bancshares, Inc.; BMO Financial Corp.; Capital One Financial Corporation; Citigroup, Inc.; Comerica Incorporated; Discover Financial Services; Fifth Third Bancorp; The Goldman Sachs Group, Inc.; HSBC North America Holdings Inc.; Huntington Bancorporation Incorporated; JPMorgan Chase & Co.; Keycorp; M&T Bank Corporation; Morgan Stanley; Northern Trust Corporation; The PNC Financial Services Group, Inc.; RBS Citizens Financial Group, Inc.; Regions Financial Corporation; Santander Holdings USA, Inc.; State Street Corporation; SunTrust Banks, Inc.; U.S. Bancorp; UnionBanCal Corp.; Wells Fargo & Co.; and Zions Bancorporation. In 2013, the Financial Stability Oversight Council designated three non-bank financial companies for consolidated supervision by the Federal Reserve and enhanced prudential standards: American International Group, Inc., General Electric Capital Corporation, Inc., and Prudential Financial, Inc.

- **Completion of the ResCap bankruptcy:** In December 2013, the bankruptcy of Ally Financial's ResCap subsidiary was substantially resolved.[28] The Bankruptcy Court entered an order confirming a bankruptcy plan on December 11, 2013, which became effective on December 17, 2013. The final bankruptcy agreement included a settlement, which the bankruptcy court judge had approved in June 2013, releasing Ally Financial from any and all legal claims by ResCap and, subject to certain exceptions, all other third parties, in exchange for $2.1 billion in cash from Ally Financial and its insurers.[29] According to Ally Financial, its mortgage operations were a significant portion of its operations and were conducted primarily through ResCap. With the completion of the ResCap settlement, Ally Financial largely exited the mortgage origination and servicing business.

Other regulatory issues were also resolved in 2013, which removed additional elements of uncertainty, according to Treasury officials and rating agency analyses. In December 2013, Ally Financial received approval from the Federal Reserve for its filing to elect financial holding company status. As a bank holding company that had not made an election to be treated as a financial holding company, Ally Financial would have been restricted from carrying out certain nonbanking activities, such as insurance underwriting. However, when Ally Financial (then known as GMAC) received approval to become a bank holding company in 2008, Ally Financial was able to continue to offer certain existing insurance services on a temporary basis under the authority of section 4(a)(2) of the Bank Holding Company Act of 1956.[30] The authority expired on the fifth anniversary of the date that Ally Financial became a bank holding company, or December 24, 2013. Gaining financial holding company status enabled Ally Financial to continue to offer its insurance and auction lines of business, according to Ally Financial. Further, in December 2013

---

[28]See Order Confirming Second Amended Joint Chapter 11 Plan Proposed by Residential Capital, LLC, et al., and the Official Committee of Unsecured Creditors, *In re Residential Capital, LLC*, No. 1:12-12020 (Bankr. S.D.N.Y. Dec. 11, 2013); Notice of Entry of Confirmation Order Confirming the Second Amended Joint Chapter 11 Plan Proposed by Residential Capital, LLC, et al., and the Official Committee of Unsecured Creditors and Occurrence of Effective Date, *In re Residential Capital, LLC*, No. 1:12-12020 (Bankr. S.D.N.Y. Dec. 17, 2013).

[29]See Order Confirming Second Amended Joint Chapter 11 Plan Proposed by Residential Capital, LLC, et al., and the Official Committee of Unsecured Creditors at 55, 62, *In re Residential Capital, LLC*, No. 1:12-12020 (Bankr. S.D.N.Y. Dec. 11, 2013).

[30]Pub. L. No. 84-511, § 4(a)(2), 70 Stat. 133, 135 (codified at 12 U.S.C. § 1843(a)(2)).

Ally Financial settled allegations of violations of the Equal Credit Opportunity Act by paying $98 million relating to the execution of consent orders issued by the Department of Justice and the Consumer Financial Protection Bureau.[31]

Since December 2013, Treasury's Ownership Share in Ally Financial Has Declined at an Accelerated Pace

After the legal and regulatory developments in late 2013, the pace of Treasury's reduction in its ownership share of Ally Financial accelerated. From December 2013 through June 2014, Treasury reduced its ownership share of Ally Financial by almost 80 percent (see fig. 1). In November 2013, Ally Financial made cash payments totaling $5.9 billion to repurchase all remaining mandatory convertible preferred shares outstanding and terminate an existing share adjustment provision.[32] Additionally, Ally Financial issued $1.3 billion of common equity to third-party investors, reducing Treasury's ownership share from 74 to 63 percent. In January 2014, Treasury completed a private placement of Ally Financial common stock valued at approximately $3 billion, further reducing Treasury's ownership share of Ally Financial to 37 percent. According to Treasury, the decision to undertake a private placement at that time was based on market conditions, as well as information Treasury received about increasing investor interest from the underwriter of two previous private placements of Ally Financial shares—the $1.3 billion private placement Ally Financial completed in November 2013 and an approximate $900 million private offering by GM of its remaining Ally Financial stock in December 2013. These transactions contributed to building an investor base for the stock, according to Treasury and Ally Financial.

[31]Consent Order, *United States v. Ally Financial Inc. and Ally Bank,* No. 2:13-cv-15180, (E.D. Mich. Dec. 23, 2013); Consent Order, *In the Matter of Ally Financial Inc.; and Ally Bank,* File No. 2013-CFPB-0010 (Dec. 20, 2013). The settlement required Ally Financial to provide $80 million in compensation to victims of discrimination and $18 million to the Consumer Financial Protection Bureau's Civil Penalty Fund.

[32]The share adjustment provision provided Treasury with the right to purchase additional shares of Ally Financial common stock.

Figure 1: Treasury's Ownership Share of Ally Financial, 2010-2014

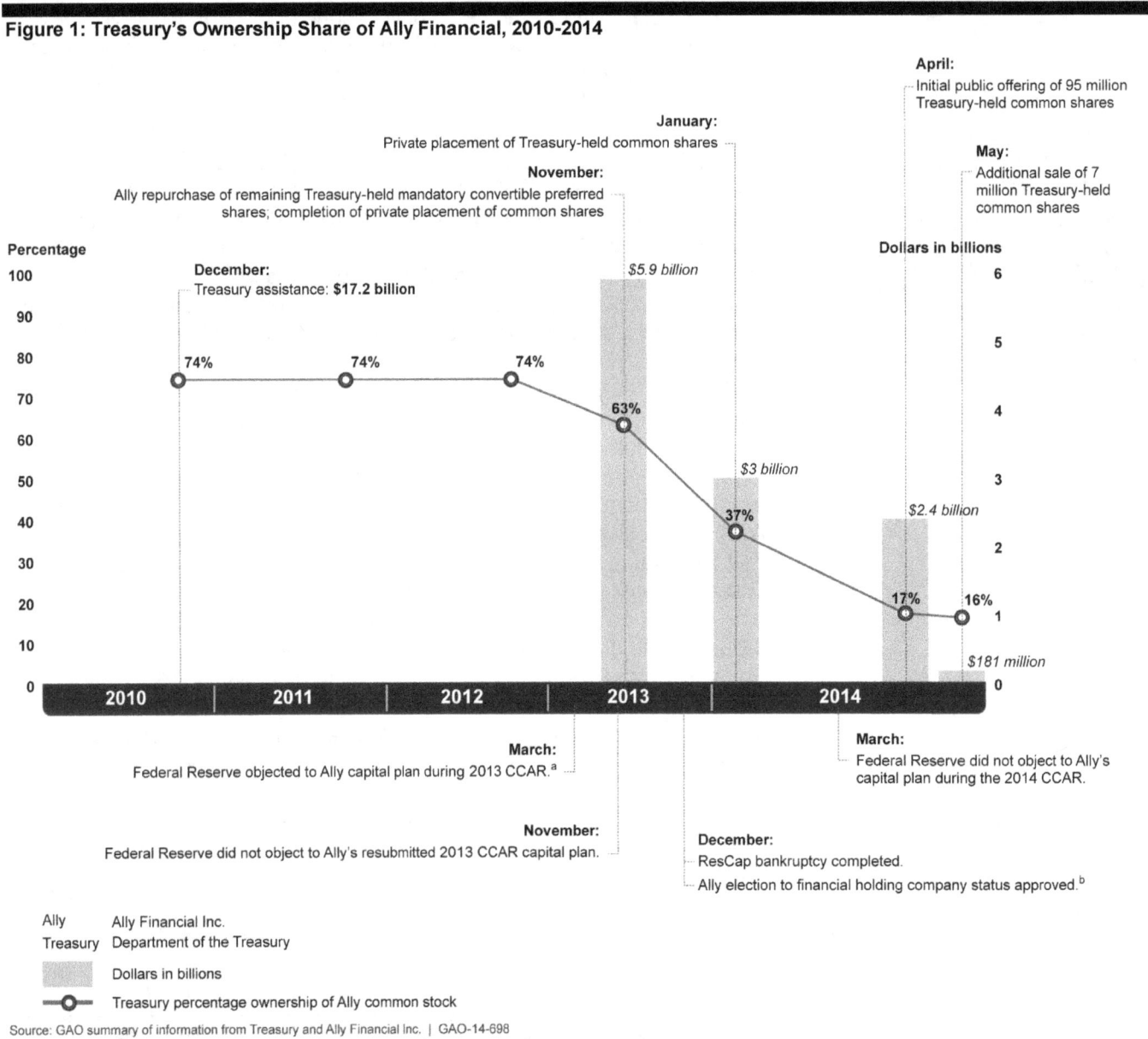

Ally   Ally Financial Inc.
Treasury Department of the Treasury

☐ Dollars in billions

━O━ Treasury percentage ownership of Ally common stock

Source: GAO summary of information from Treasury and Ally Financial Inc. | GAO-14-698

Notes:

[a]CCAR—Comprehensive Capital Analysis and Review—is an annual Federal Reserve assessment of the internal capital planning process and capital adequacy of large, complex U.S. bank holding companies.

[b]Financial holding company status enables Ally Financial to continue to engage in insurance underwriting and other nonbanking activities.

Treasury said the positive results of the March 2014 Federal Reserve stress test and CCAR contributed to the decision to further reduce its ownership share. The day after the release of the CCAR results in March 2014, Treasury announced that it would sell Ally Financial common stock in an initial public offering (IPO) and in April 2014, completed the IPO of 95 million Treasury shares at $25 per share. The $2.4 billion sale reduced Treasury's ownership share to approximately 17 percent. Following the IPO, Ally Financial became a publicly held company. In May 2014, Treasury received $181 million from the sale of additional shares after underwriters exercised the option to purchase an additional 7 million shares from Treasury at the IPO price. This additional sale reduced Treasury's ownership share to approximately 16 percent. As of June 30, 2014, Treasury had received $17.8 billion in sales proceeds and interest and dividend payments on its total assistance to Ally Financial of $17.2 billion.[33]

Based on the stock prices, as of June 30, 2014, Treasury's remaining investment in Ally Financial, which consists of common stock, was valued at almost $1.8 billion. Treasury stated that it would like to divest its ownership stake in Ally Financial in a manner that balances the speed of recovery with maximizing returns for taxpayers. Treasury officials told us that Treasury does not have a specific date by which it intends to fully divest from the company, but that its decision on timing will be based on market conditions. These market conditions, in part, will reflect Ally Financial's financial performance.

---

[33]In addition to repayments on the initial investment, Treasury has received dividends and other income from Ally Financial worth approximately $4.6 billion. For example, Treasury received a 9.0 percent fixed dividend annually from Ally Financial for the mandatory convertible preferred shares held until November 2013.

GAO-14-698 Troubled Asset Relief Program

Ally Financial's Business Structure Has Been Evolving and Its Financial Condition Has Continued to Stabilize

Since 2013, Ally Financial has continued its evolution into a publicly held, monoline finance company in the automotive sector with an Internet bank. Ally Financial's financial condition continued to stabilize in late 2013 and early 2014 and the company raised significant levels of common equity through private and public share offerings. According to recent rating agency analyses, Ally Financial is competitive in automotive financing, particularly in the floor-plan business segment, but faces potential competitive challenges, such as its reliance on GM and Chrysler auto financing relationships.[34]

Ally Financial's Evolving Business Structure

Ally Financial's business structure has been simplified and clarified over the past year, according to rating agency analyses and federal regulatory officials. Specifically, the completion of the ResCap bankruptcy marked the company's exit from the mortgage origination and servicing business. Ally Financial became a financial holding company in December 2013, which, according to the company, enabled it to retain its insurance and auction lines of business and maintain its full suite of products for dealers. Ally Financial also completed sales of its European and Latin American automotive finance operations to GM Financial, GM's captive financing company, and its Canadian operations to Royal Bank of Canada.[35] Ally Financial expects to complete GM Financial's acquisition of its remaining international operation—its China joint venture, in which the company is a 40 percent owner—in 2014, subject to government approvals in China.

Ally Financial's Financial Condition Has Continued to Stabilize

Since our last review in 2013, Ally Financial's financial performance has continued to stabilize as illustrated by multiple capital, profitability, and liquidity measures. Taking into account the resolution of ResCap, the sale of international operations, and other factors, the three largest credit rating agencies upgraded Ally Financial's ratings, although the ratings remain below investment grade.

---

[34]As discussed previously, floor-plan, or wholesale, lending is a form of retail goods inventory financing in which each loan advance is made against a specific piece of collateral.

[35]As we reported in GAO-14-6, in 2009, GM acquired AmeriCredit Corporation (AmeriCredit), a subprime automobile finance company, to serve its subprime customers. AmeriCredit was renamed GM Financial and made a wholly owned subsidiary of GM. Its target lending market is consumers who have difficulty securing automobile financing from banks and credit unions.

Capital Position	Ally Financial's capital position has remained the same or improved since 2009—the year it became subject to regulatory and reporting requirements following its conversion to a bank holding company in December 2008. Capital can be measured in several ways, but we focused on tier 1 capital because it is currently the strongest form of capital (see table 1). We examined Ally Financial's tier 1 capital ratio and tier 1 leverage ratio and compared them to minimums required under the Federal Reserve's capital adequacy guidelines for bank holding companies. We also examined Ally Financial's tier 1 common ratio. The Federal Reserve has long held the view that bank holding companies generally should operate with capital positions well above the minimum regulatory capital ratios, with the amount of capital held commensurate with a bank holding company's risk profile.[36]

- **Tier 1 capital and tier 1 common capital ratios:** Higher tier 1 capital and common capital ratios may indicate that a bank holding company is in a better position to absorb financial losses. A tier 1 capital ratio measures tier 1 capital as a percentage of risk-weighted assets. As shown in table 1, Ally Financial's tier 1 capital ratio increased from 2009 to 2010 but has declined slightly since 2011. Federal Reserve Capital Adequacy Guidelines require bank holding companies to have a tier 1 risk-based capital ratio of at least 4 percent.[37] Ally Financial's tier 1 capital ratio exceeded the required minimum each year from 2009 through 2013. In 2013, Ally Financial reported that the tier 1 capital ratio declined, in part, because of the repurchase of Treasury's mandatory convertible preferred shares, which qualified as tier 1 capital. A tier 1 common capital ratio measures common capital—that is, the common equity component of tier 1 capital as a share of risk-weighted assets. Ally Financial's tier 1 common ratio has increased

---

[36]Capital Plans, 76 Fed. Reg. 74631, 74632 (Dec. 1, 2011); see also Capital Adequacy Guidelines for Bank Holding Companies, 12 CFR § 225, Appendix A, § I.

[37]12 C.F.R. 225, Appendix A, § IV.A. Federal Reserve Capital Adequacy Guidelines require bank holding companies to have a minimum tier 1 risk-based capital ratio of 6 percent to be considered well capitalized. 12 C.F.R. § 225.2(r)(1)(ii).

from 4.85 percent at the end of 2009 to 8.84 percent at the end of 2013.[38]

- **Tier 1 leverage ratio:** A tier 1 leverage ratio shows the relationship between a banking organization's core capital and total assets. The tier 1 leverage ratio is calculated by dividing the tier 1 capital by the firm's average total consolidated assets. Generally, a larger tier 1 leverage ratio indicates that a company is less risky because it has more equity to absorb losses in the value of its assets. As shown in table 1, Ally Financial's leverage ratio has been reduced by 20 percent since 2009 but remains well above the regulatory minimum guideline of 3 or 4 percent, depending on the bank holding company's composite rating.[39]

Table 1: Ally Financial Capital Ratios, 2009-2013

	2009	2010	2011	2012	2013
Tier 1 capital ratio	14.15%	15.00%	13.71%	13.13%	11.79%
Tier 1 common capital ratio[a]	4.85	8.57	7.57	6.98	8.84
Tier 1 leverage ratio	12.70	13.05	11.50	11.16	10.23

Source: SNL. | GAO-14-698

[a]Federal Reserve Capital Adequacy Guidelines do not require a minimum tier 1 common capital ratio. However, companies subject to the Federal Reserve's capital plan rule must develop a capital plan that demonstrates the company's ability to meet a tier 1 common ratio above 5 percent under stressed conditions. See 12 CFR 225.8(d)(2) (i)(B).

Profitability

Ally Financial's profitability continued to improve in early 2014, after declining in the fourth quarter of 2013 because of certain one-time expenses, as described later. We examined several measures of

---

[38]This ratio is not a minimum ratio outside of the Federal Reserve's CCAR. Ally Financial will become subject to a new regulatory capital framework beginning January 1, 2015. Once fully phased in, the new rules will require that Ally Financial maintain a minimum common equity tier 1 risk-based capital ratio of 4.5 percent, a minimum tier 1 risk-based capital ratio of 6 percent, and a minimum total risk-based capital ratio of 8 percent. The new capital rules also revise the eligibility criteria for regulatory capital instruments. Regulatory Capital Rules: Regulatory Capital, Implementation of Basel III, Capital Adequacy, Transition Provisions, Prompt Corrective Action, Standardized Approach for Risk-weighted Assets, Market Discipline and Disclosure Requirements, Advanced Approaches Risk-Based Capital Rule, and Market Risk Capital Rule; Final Rule, 78 Fed. Reg. 62018 (Oct. 11, 2013).

[39]12 C.F.R. 225, Appendix D, § II.

profitability, including net income (loss), net interest spread, return on assets, and nonperforming asset ratio.

- **Net income (loss):** Ally Financial suffered a net loss in 2009 of $10 billion, but has reported net income for 4 of the last 5 years. As shown in figure 2, the 2009 loss was driven by substantial losses in its mortgage business operating unit. Ally Financial reported net income of $361 million in 2013, down from net income of $1.2 billion in 2012. The company attributed the decline to circumstances including a tax valuation adjustment of $1 billion in 2012; the 2013 payment of $1.4 billion as part of the ResCap settlement agreement; and the $98 million payment in connection with the Department of Justice and Consumer Financial Protection Bureau consent orders.

Figure 2: Ally Financial Net Income (Loss) by Operating Unit, 2009-2013

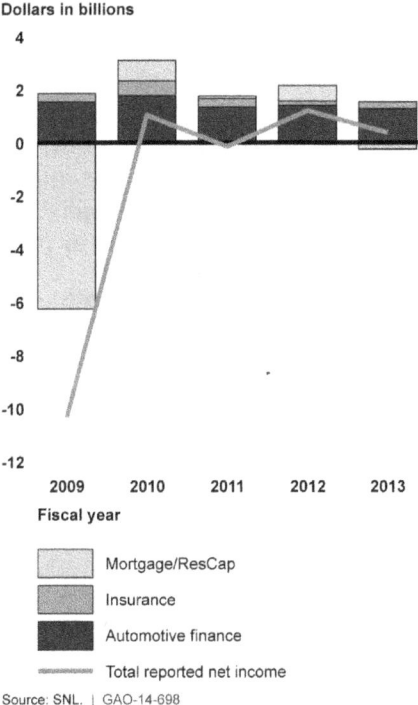

Source: SNL. | GAO-14-698

Notes: Data are the most recent reported values in Ally Financial reports on Form 10-K. Ally Financial reported a net loss in 2011 due to the accrual of foreclosure-related expenses. Total reported net income does not always equal the sum of the three operating units because of the exclusion of "other" income.

- **Net interest spread:** The net interest spread is the difference between the average rate on total interest-earning assets and the average rate on total interest-bearing liabilities, excluding discontinued operations for the period. In general, the larger the spread, the more a company is earning. Ally Financial's net interest spread increased from a reported 0.31 percent at the end of 2009 to 1.75 percent at the end of 2013, meaning that Ally Financial is earning more interest on its assets than it is paying interest on its liabilities (see table 2).[40]

- **Return on assets (ROA):** ROA is calculated by dividing a company's net income by its total assets. It is an indication of how profitable a company is relative to its total assets and gives an idea of management's efficiency in using its assets to generate earnings. A higher ROA suggests that a company is using its assets efficiently. Ally Financial reported improved ROA from 2009 to 2013, with a reported negative 5.81 percent ROA for 2009 and a positive 0.23 percent in 2013.

- **Nonperforming asset ratio:** This ratio measures asset quality by dividing the value of nonperforming assets by the value of total assets. The lower the ratio, the fewer poorly performing assets a company holds. Ally Financial's nonperforming asset ratio fell from 4.36 percent in 2009 to 1.19 percent in 2013 (see table 2).

Table 2: Net Interest Spread, Return on Assets, and Nonperforming Asset Ratio for Ally Financial, 2009-2013

	2009	2010	2011	2012	2013
Net interest spread	0.31	0.81	0.69	1.18	1.75
Return on assets	(5.81)	0.58	(0.09)	0.65	0.23
Nonperforming asset ratio	4.36	3.46	2.69	1.06	1.19

Source: GAO analysis of Ally Financial and SNL data. | GAO-14-698

Liquidity, Bank Deposits, and Cash Flow

Ally Financial's liquidity position generally has stabilized since 2009. To examine Ally Financial's liquidity position, we examined the company's total liquidity ratio, bank deposits, and operating cash flow.

---

[40]Ally Financial Inc. Annual Report (Form 10-K) (Dec. 31, 2013). Ally Financial restated its net interest spread figures for prior years in its 2013 Form 10-K.

- **Total liquidity ratio:** Liquidity ratios measure a bank's total liquid assets against its total liabilities. Generally, the ratios indicate a bank's ability to sell assets quickly to cover short-term debts—with a higher ratio providing a larger margin of safety.[41] Overall, Ally Financial's liquidity ratio remained fairly stable from the third quarter of 2009 through the fourth quarter of 2013 (see fig. 3). Declines in liquidity levels in 2012 and 2013 were associated with repayments of government assistance. For example, according to Ally Financial, the decline in liquidity in 2013 was due to the repurchase of the Treasury mandatory convertible preferred shares and the redemption of certain high-coupon, callable debt. For the quarter ending March 31, 2014, Ally Financial reported a total liquidity ratio of 16.01 percent.

---

[41]In February 2014, the Federal Reserve issued a final rule to implement certain enhanced prudential standards under the Dodd-Frank Act for large bank holding companies. Enhanced Prudential Standards for Bank Holding Companies and Foreign Banking Organizations; Final Rule. 79 Fed. Reg. 17240 (Mar. 27, 2014) (codified at 12 C.F.R. pt. 252). In its annual report (Form 10-K), Ally Financial reported that the final rule will, among other things, require the company to maintain a buffer of unencumbered highly liquid assets to meet projected net cash outflows for 30 days over the range of liquidity stress scenarios used in internal stress tests and to comply with a number of risk management and governance requirements, including liquidity risk management standards. The final rule has a general compliance date of January 1, 2015. 12 C.F.R. § 252.31(c).

GAO-14-698 Troubled Asset Relief Program

Figure 3: Ally Financial Liquidity Ratio, September 2009-March 2014

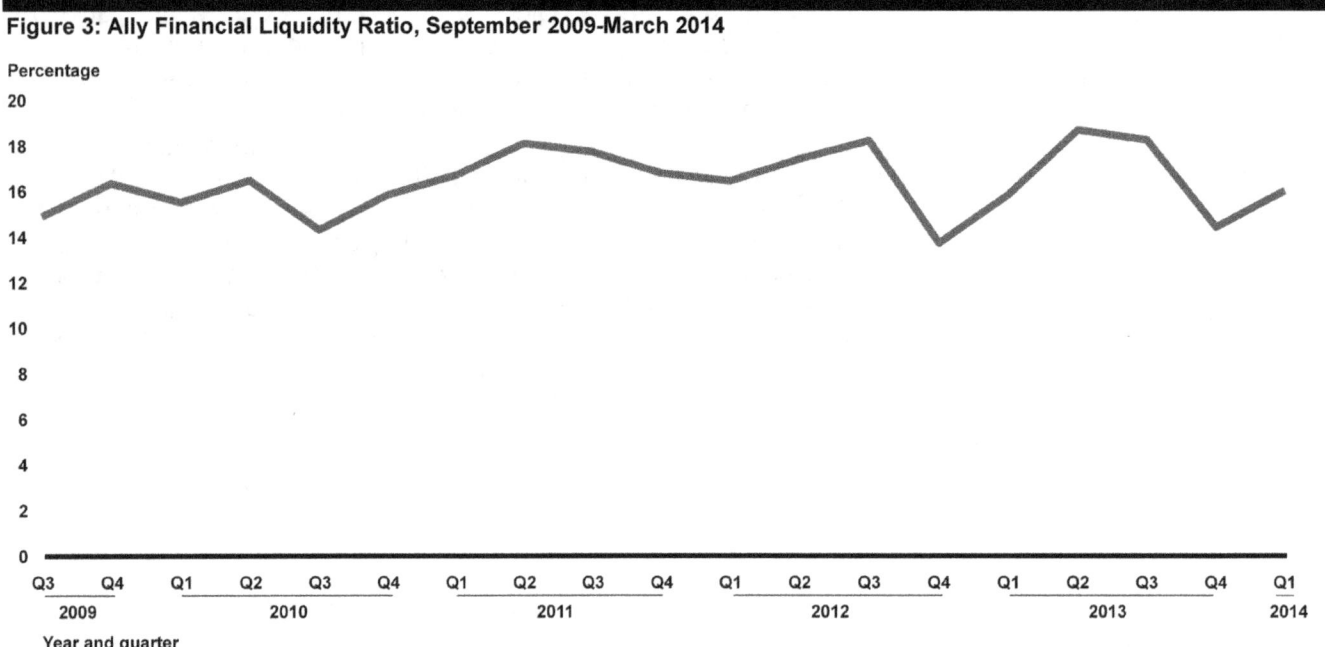

Percentage

Year and quarter

Source: SNL. | GAO-14-698

- **Bank deposits:** Bank deposits are the funds that consumers and businesses place with a bank, and growth in deposits is an important factor in the bank's liquidity position. From December 2008 to March 2014, deposits at Ally Bank, Ally Financial's Internet bank, grew almost 190 percent, from $19.3 billion to $55.9 billion, of which approximately $45.2 billion were retail (consumer) deposits. Deposits accounted for 43 percent of Ally Financial's total funding as of the first quarter of 2014, providing the company with a low-cost source of funding that is less sensitive to interest rate changes and market volatility than other sources of funding.

- **Operating cash flow:** From the first quarter of 2010 through the third quarter of 2013, Ally Financial generated positive cash flow from operating activities (see fig. 4). Since the third quarter of 2013, cash flows have varied, with Ally reporting negative cash flow in the fourth quarter of 2013 and positive cash flow at the end of the first quarter of 2014. According to Ally Financial, 2013 declines in operating cash flow (compared with the prior year) were driven by the settlement of

GAO-14-698 Troubled Asset Relief Program

derivative transactions, but were partially offset by sales and repayments of mortgage and automotive loans.[42]

Figure 4: Ally Financial Operating Cash Flow, September 2009-March 2014

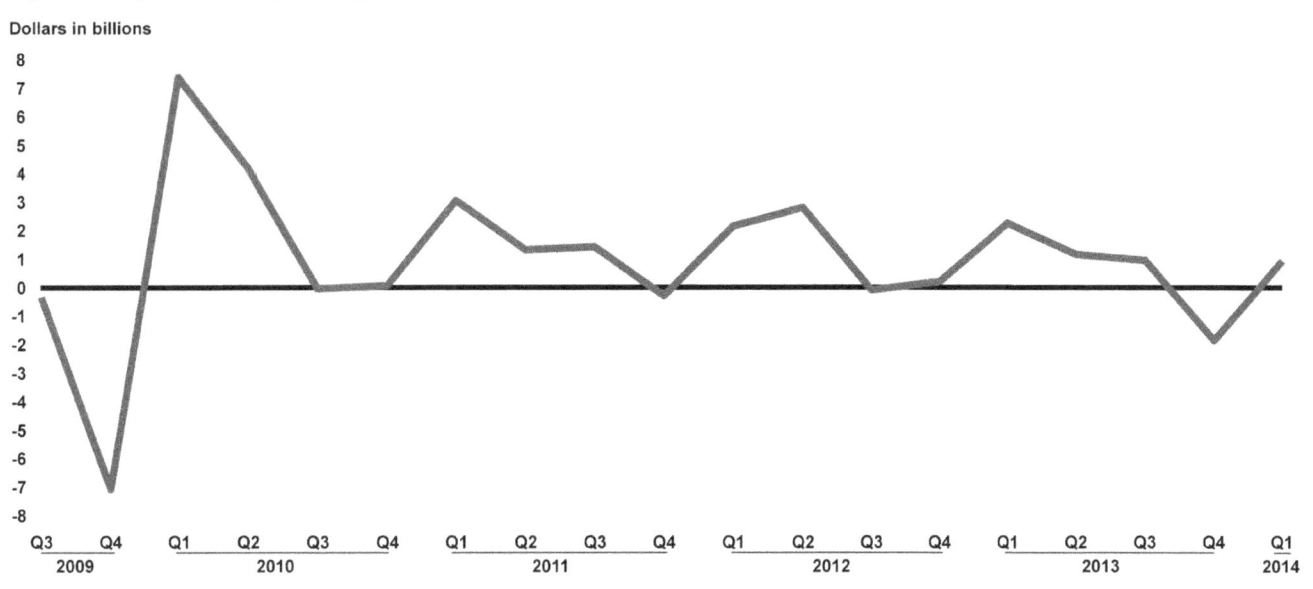

Source: SNL. | GAO-14-698

Ally Financial's changing financial condition is reflected in its credit rating. Although Ally's credit rating remains below investment grade, its long-term credit rating with the three largest credit rating agencies has been upgraded multiple times since 2009. Most recently, Ally's long-term ratings with Moody's, Standard and Poor's, and Fitch Ratings were upgraded to Ba3, BB, and BB+, respectively.

---

[42]According to Ally Financial, the decrease was primarily due to higher cash outflows to settle derivatives during the year ended December 31, 2013. During 2013, Ally Financial completed the sale of its mortgage servicing rights assets and effectively exited the mortgage origination and servicing business. Further, the wind-down and ultimate termination of mortgage-related derivative activity was a driver of the operating cash outflows for the year ended December 31, 2013. These wind-down activities occurred throughout 2013 and were not isolated to the fourth quarter.

Ally Financial Continues to Face Competitive Challenges

According to rating agency analyses, Ally Financial is a strong competitor in automotive financing, although the company faces competitive challenges. Analysts have said that Ally Financial is competitive in automotive financing, particularly in the floor-plan business segment. In addition, as mentioned previously in this report, Ally Bank has continued to increase its level of retail deposits.

Analysts have pointed to potential competitive challenges for Ally Financial, such as its reliance on GM and Chrysler automotive financing relationships. As we previously reported, GM and Chrysler have established captive financing units.[43] Ally's exclusive lending relationships with GM and Chrysler have ended as the two automakers have begun to rely on their captive financing units. For example, the agreement between GM and Ally Financial on dealer and consumer lending was revised in early 2014. Among other changes, Ally Financial no longer enjoys exclusivity with regard to GM lending arrangements.[44] The captive financing units of GM and Chrysler have begun to increase their financing activities. However, according to Ally Financial representatives, the company is the only automotive finance company that offers a suite of

---

[43]As we previously reported, according to GM officials, the purpose of GM Financial is to drive incremental GM automobile sales by providing funding for GM dealers and consumers. In 2013, GM Financial increased its overall assets by purchasing Ally Financial's international assets, including the dealer financing arrangements in these countries. In February 2013, Chrysler announced that it had entered into an agreement with Santander Consumer USA Inc., a subsidiary of Banco Santander, S.A., that specializes in subprime automotive financing, to provide a full spectrum of automotive financing services to Chrysler Group customers and dealers under the name of Chrysler Capital. Under the 10-year, private-label agreement, Santander Consumer USA was to establish a separate lending operation dedicated to providing financial services under the Chrysler Capital name, including financing for retail loans and leases, new and used vehicle inventory, dealership construction, real estate, working capital, and revolving lines of credit. The agreement grants Santander Consumer USA the right to a minimum percentage of Chrysler's subvention—subsidy or financial support—volume and the right to use the Chrysler Capital name for automobile loan and lease offerings. Santander Consumer USA also will provide loans to Chrysler dealers to finance inventory, working capital, and capital improvements. On May 1, 2013, Chrysler Capital started its lending operations.

[44]Ally Financial reported that it entered into a new automotive financing agreement with GM (effective Mar. 1, 2014) that provides a general framework for dealer and consumer financing related to GM vehicles, as well as Ally Financial's ongoing participation in GM subvention programs. The agreement does not provide Ally with any exclusivity or similar privileges related to the financing of GM vehicles, whether through subvention programs or otherwise. As a result, the agreement does not provide the economic benefits or impose the obligations that were included in the previous agreement with GM.

products to dealers (financing, insurance, and auction services) and as a result, the company expects to continue to be competitive in this segment. Moreover, Ally Financial representatives told us that the company has been focusing more on increasing profitability than on market share—consistent with its goals as a publicly held company, which include maximizing return to shareholders. Company representatives also have said in public statements that Ally Financial has been focusing on reducing its noninterest expenses and lowering its cost of funds.

Ally Financial also faces competition from other large bank holding companies in consumer automobile financing. We compared the amount of Ally Financial consumer automobile financing with that of four large bank holding companies (Bank of America Corporation, Capital One Financial Corporation, JPMorgan Chase & Company, and Wells Fargo & Company) that reported consumer automobile loans.[45] These data do not include all types of automobile financing, such as automobile leasing and dealer financing, but only retail consumer automobile loans for the time period.[46] Most recently, in the first quarter of 2014 Wells Fargo's retail lending exceeded that of Ally Financial (see fig 5). The dollar amount of consumer automobile loans that Wells Fargo, JPMorgan Chase, and Capital One made increased from March 2011 through March 2014, while the dollar amount of Ally Financial financing has declined since the fourth quarter of 2012. According to Federal Reserve officials, this decline likely reflects the sale of the international automotive finance operations.

---

[45]These four bank holding companies are also financial holding companies.

[46]The Federal Reserve defines consumer automobile loans for bank holding company reporting purposes. They are all consumer loans extended for the purpose of purchasing new and used passenger cars and other vehicles such as minivans, vans, sport-utility vehicles, pickup trucks, and similar light trucks for personal use. These loans include both direct and indirect consumer automobile loans as well as retail installment sales papers purchased by the bank from automobile dealers. See Instructions for Preparation of Consolidated Financial Statements for Holding Companies, Reporting Form FR Y-9C, Schedule HC-Consolidated Balance Sheet.

GAO-14-698 Troubled Asset Relief Program

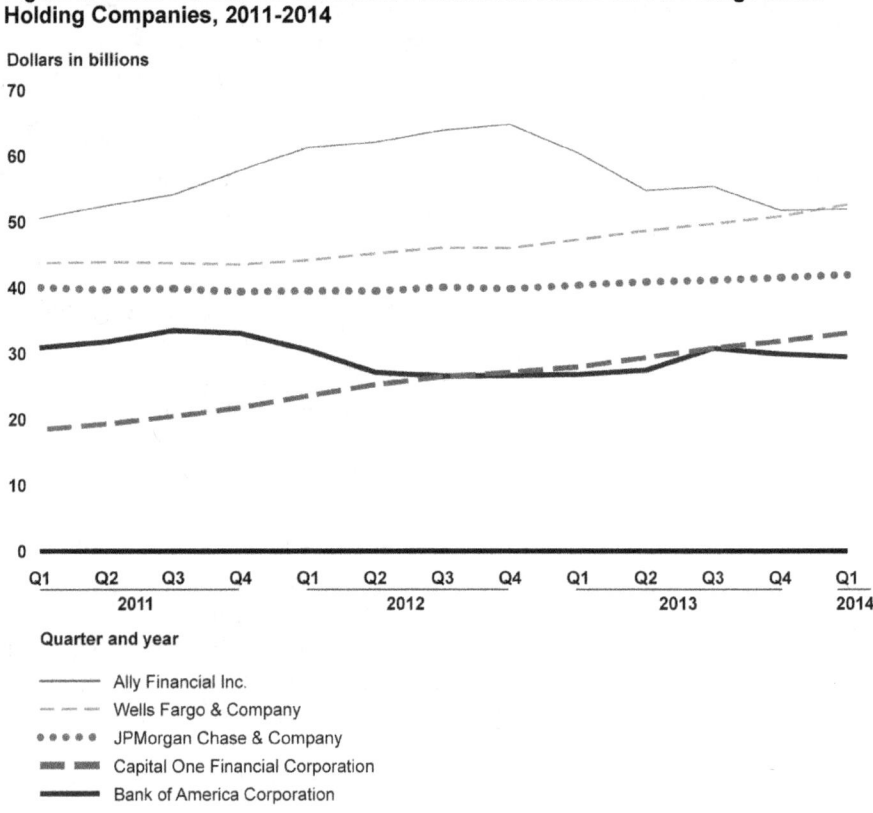

Figure 5: Dollar Amount of Consumer Automobile Loans for Five Large Bank Holding Companies, 2011-2014

Dollars in billions

Quarter and year

——— Ally Financial Inc.
– – – Wells Fargo & Company
• • • • • JPMorgan Chase & Company
▬ ▬ Capital One Financial Corporation
▬▬▬ Bank of America Corporation

Source: GAO analysis of Federal Reserve data. | GAO-14-698

Another potential area of competition is retail banking. Ally Bank, as an Internet bank, may have less of an ability to retain customers than traditional banks, according to analysts. However, as discussed previously, Ally Bank's retail deposits have continued to rise over the past year. The company expects deposits to continue to increase by about $5 billion per year for the next few years. Ally Financial representatives also told us that Ally Bank has high brand awareness and a high retention rate for products such as certificates of deposit. Ally Bank also has been able to reduce the interest rates it pays on deposits, while retaining customers. For example, Ally Bank is no longer among the top seven rate payers, according to Ally Financial representatives.

GAO-14-698 Troubled Asset Relief Program

Agency Comments

We provided a draft of this report to FDIC, the Federal Reserve, and Treasury for their review and comment. In addition, we provided a copy of the draft report to Ally Financial to help ensure the accuracy of our report. Treasury provided written comments that are reprinted in appendix II. Ally Financial provided technical comments, which we have incorporated, as appropriate. FDIC and the Federal Reserve did not provide comments.

In its written comments, Treasury generally concurred with our findings. Treasury noted that approximately $17.8 billion has been recovered to date from Ally Financial through repayments, a private placement, and an initial public offering. Treasury also noted that it will unwind its remaining ownership stake in a way that balances the speed of recovery with maximizing returns to taxpayers.

We are sending copies of this report to FDIC, the Federal Reserve, and Treasury, and the appropriate congressional committees. This report will also be available at no charge on our website at http://www.gao.gov.

If you or your staff have any questions about this report, please contact me at (202) 512-8678 or clowersa@gao.gov. Contact points for our Offices of Congressional Relations and Public Affairs may be found on the last page of this report. Key contributors to this report are listed in appendix III.

A. Nicole Clowers
Director
Financial Markets and Community Investment

List of Committees

The Honorable Barbara Mikulski
Chairwoman
The Honorable Richard C. Shelby
Vice Chairman
Committee on Appropriations
United States Senate

The Honorable Tim Johnson
Chairman
The Honorable Mike Crapo
Ranking Member
Committee on Banking, Housing, and Urban Affairs
United States Senate

The Honorable Patty Murray
Chairman
The Honorable Jeff Sessions
Ranking Member
Committee on the Budget
United States Senate

The Honorable Ron Wyden
Chairman
The Honorable Orrin G. Hatch
Ranking Member
Committee on Finance
United States Senate

The Honorable Hal Rogers
Chairman
The Honorable Nita Lowey
Ranking Member
Committee on Appropriations
House of Representatives

The Honorable Paul Ryan
Chairman
The Honorable Chris Van Hollen
Ranking Member
Committee on the Budget
House of Representatives

The Honorable Jeb Hensarling
Chairman
The Honorable Maxine Waters
Ranking Member
Committee on Financial Services
House of Representatives

The Honorable Dave Camp
Chairman
The Honorable Sander Levin
Ranking Member
Committee on Ways and Means
House of Representatives

Appendix I: Objectives, Scope, and Methodology

This report is based on our continuing analysis and monitoring of the Department of the Treasury's (Treasury) activities in implementing the Emergency Economic Stabilization Act of 2008 (EESA), which provided us with broad oversight authorities for actions taken under the Troubled Asset Relief Program (TARP).[1] This report examines (1) the status of Treasury's investments in Ally Financial Inc. (Ally Financial) as of June 30, 2014, and its efforts to wind down those investments; and (2) the financial condition of Ally Financial through March 31, 2014.

To examine the status of Treasury's investments, we reviewed TARP reports, which included monthly reports to Congress and daily TARP updates regarding the Automotive Industry Financing Program (AIFP) program data. Using the AIFP program data, we analyzed Treasury's equity ownership and recovery of funds in Ally Financial for the time period from January 2009 through June 2014. We have previously assessed the reliability of the AIFP program data from Treasury. For example, we tested the Office of Financial Stability's internal controls over financial reporting as they related to our annual audit of the office's financial statements and found the information to be sufficiently reliable based on the results of our audit of the TARP financial statements for fiscal years 2009—2013. AIFP was included in these financial audits.[2] In addition, for this review, we reviewed the data for completeness and obvious errors such as outliers. Based on this review, we determined that the data were sufficiently reliable for our purposes.

To analyze Treasury's efforts to wind down its investments in Ally Financial, we reviewed Treasury documentation relating to its exit from Ally Financial. We reviewed Ally Financial regulatory filings, including Securities and Exchange Commission (SEC) filings; and publicly available reports from the Board of Governors of the Federal Reserve System (Federal Reserve) on the Dodd-Frank Wall Street Reform and Consumer Protection Act (Dodd-Frank Act) stress test and capital plan analysis, *Dodd-Frank Act Stress Test 2014: Supervisory Stress Test Methodology and Results*; and *Comprehensive Capital Analysis and*

---

[1]Pub. L. No. 110-343, § 116, 122 Stat. 3765, 3783 (codified at 12 U.S.C. § 5226).

[2]EESA, which was signed into law on October 3, 2008, established the Office of Financial Stability within Treasury and provided it with broad, flexible authorities to buy or guarantee troubled mortgage-related assets or any other financial instruments necessary to stabilize the financial markets. § 101(a), 122 Stat. at 3767 (codified at 12 U.S.C. § 5211(a)).

Review 2014: Assessment Framework and Results.[3] In addition, we
interviewed officials from Treasury, the Federal Reserve, the Federal
Deposit Insurance Corporation (FDIC), and representatives from Ally
Financial.

To assess the financial condition of Ally Financial, we measured the
institution's capital ratios, net income, net interest spread margin, return
on assets, nonperforming asset ratio, liquidity ratio, bank deposits, and
operating cash flow, generally from 2009 through the first quarter (March
31) of 2014. We obtained these data from SNL Financial, a provider of
financial information. We have determined that SNL Financial data are
sufficiently reliable for past reports, and we reviewed past GAO data
reliability assessments to ensure that we, in all material respects, used
the data in a similar manner and for similar purposes. We also reviewed
reports by several credit rating agencies on how they rate Ally Financial's
financial strength. Although we have reported on actions needed to
improve the oversight of rating agencies, we included these ratings
because the ratings are widely used by Ally Financial, Treasury, and
market participants. To obtain information on the financial ratios and
indicators used in the analyses of Ally Financial's financial condition, we
reviewed relevant documentation and interviewed officials from FDIC, the
Federal Reserve, Treasury, and representatives from Ally Financial. For
the comparison of retail (consumer) automotive lending for five large bank
holding companies, including Ally Financial, we used Federal Reserve
regulatory filings (Form FR-Y9C). For each data source we reviewed the
data for completeness and obvious errors and determined that these data
were sufficiently reliable for our purposes.

We conducted this performance audit from March 2014 to August 2014 in
accordance with generally accepted government auditing standards.
Those standards require that we plan and perform the audit to obtain
sufficient, appropriate evidence to provide a reasonable basis for our
findings and conclusions based on our audit objectives. We believe that
the evidence obtained provides a reasonable basis for our findings and
conclusions based on our audit objectives.

---

[3]Pub. L. No. 111-203, 124 Stat. 1376 (2010).

DEPARTMENT OF THE TREASURY
WASHINGTON, D.C. 20220

ASSISTANT SECRETARY

July 18, 2014

Nikki Clowers
Director
Financial Markets and Community Investment
U.S. Government Accountability Office
441 G Street, NW
Washington, D.C. 20548

Dear Ms. Clowers:

The Department of the Treasury (Treasury) welcomes the opportunity to provide comments to your draft report on Treasury's investment in Ally Financial (Ally), entitled *Government's Exposure to Ally Financial Lessens as Treasury's Ownership Share Declines* (Draft Report).

GAO's Draft Report provides constructive insight on Treasury's efforts to exit Ally in a manner that balances speed of recovery with maximizing returns for taxpayers. As part of the Automotive Industry Financing Program under the Troubled Asset Relief Program (TARP), Treasury invested a total of $17.2 billion in Ally (formerly GMAC). Founded as GM's captive finance subsidiary in 1919, Ally has been the primary source of financing for GM's dealers and consumers for over 90 years. Treasury determined that without government assistance, Ally would have been forced to suspend financing lines to creditworthy dealerships, leaving them unable to purchase automobile inventory for their lots.

Since 2011, Ally has executed a substantial restructuring plan, and transformed itself into a viable and profitable auto lending business that continues to support the auto industry recovery. To date, Treasury has recovered approximately $17.8 billion from Ally, approximately $600 million more than was originally invested in the company, through repayments, a private placement, and an initial public offering. As the Draft Report points out, Treasury will divest its remaining ownership stake in Ally in a manner that balances the speed of recovery with maximizing returns for taxpayers.

Treasury values GAO's review and analysis of its investment in Ally, and we look forward to continuing to work with you and your team on these important matters.

Sincerely,

Timothy J. Bowler
Acting Assistant Secretary for Financial Stability

Appendix III: Contact and Staff Acknowledgments

GAO Contact	A. Nicole Clowers, (202) 512-8678 or clowersa@gao.gov
Staff Acknowledgments	In addition to the contact named above, Karen Tremba (Assistant Director), Catherine Gelb (Analyst-in-Charge), Bethany Benitez, William Chatlos, Risto Laboski, Terence Lam, Barbara Roesmann, and Jena Sinkfield made significant contributions to this report.

GAO's Mission	The Government Accountability Office, the audit, evaluation, and investigative arm of Congress, exists to support Congress in meeting its constitutional responsibilities and to help improve the performance and accountability of the federal government for the American people. GAO examines the use of public funds; evaluates federal programs and policies; and provides analyses, recommendations, and other assistance to help Congress make informed oversight, policy, and funding decisions. GAO's commitment to good government is reflected in its core values of accountability, integrity, and reliability.
Obtaining Copies of GAO Reports and Testimony	The fastest and easiest way to obtain copies of GAO documents at no cost is through GAO's website (http://www.gao.gov). Each weekday afternoon, GAO posts on its website newly released reports, testimony, and correspondence. To have GAO e-mail you a list of newly posted products, go to http://www.gao.gov and select "E-mail Updates."
Order by Phone	The price of each GAO publication reflects GAO's actual cost of production and distribution and depends on the number of pages in the publication and whether the publication is printed in color or black and white. Pricing and ordering information is posted on GAO's website, http://www.gao.gov/ordering.htm.
	Place orders by calling (202) 512-6000, toll free (866) 801-7077, or TDD (202) 512-2537.
	Orders may be paid for using American Express, Discover Card, MasterCard, Visa, check, or money order. Call for additional information.
Connect with GAO	Connect with GAO on Facebook, Flickr, Twitter, and YouTube. Subscribe to our RSS Feeds or E-mail Updates. Listen to our Podcasts. Visit GAO on the web at www.gao.gov.
To Report Fraud, Waste, and Abuse in Federal Programs	Contact: Website: http://www.gao.gov/fraudnet/fraudnet.htm E-mail: fraudnet@gao.gov Automated answering system: (800) 424-5454 or (202) 512-7470
Congressional Relations	Katherine Siggerud, Managing Director, siggerudk@gao.gov, (202) 512-4400, U.S. Government Accountability Office, 441 G Street NW, Room 7125, Washington, DC 20548
Public Affairs	Chuck Young, Managing Director, youngc1@gao.gov, (202) 512-4800 U.S. Government Accountability Office, 441 G Street NW, Room 7149 Washington, DC 20548

Please Print on Recycled Paper.

www.ingramcontent.com/pod-product-compliance
Lightning Source LLC
Chambersburg PA
CBHW080735290526
45790CB00008B/3197